Paddling by the Shore

Paddling by the Shore

Hymns of Kim Fabricius

Kim Fabricius

Foreword by
Benjamin Myers

RESOURCE *Publications* · Eugene, Oregon

PADDLING BY THE SHORE
Hymns of Kim Fabricius

Resource Publications
An Imprint of Wipf and Stock Publishers
199 W. 8th Ave., Suite 3
Eugene, OR 97401

www.wipfandstock.com

ISBN 13: 978-1-4982-0006-6

Manufactured in the U.S.A.   02/13/2015

Thanks, Mom—you were right—for making me do my homework; and kisses, sweet Scarlett Grace, for keeping Grandpa silly.

I was like a boy playing on the sea-shore,
whilst the great ocean of truth lay all undiscovered before me.

– ISAAC NEWTON

Contents

Preface

IT ALL STARTED ONE week when I had finished writing my sermon and began selecting the hymns for an evening service at which I would be preaching on the Bible. In the sermon I imagined a conversation among the four evangelists, who had been shortlisted by a heavenly committee before which they were now appearing, each arguing his case for *his* particular gospel to be *the* authoritative gospel. This trope, stolen and adapted from the approach George Caird took in his *New Testament Theology*[1], expressed an understanding of the Bible that I intended to commend to my congregation, namely, that scripture is a conversation which its readers overhear, engage, and discuss in those ongoing and often disputatious conversations we call "tradition."

There was only one problem: in the hymn books available to me I could not find a hymn that would "bring it all together" to conclude our worship. At the same time, I couldn't get out of my head the phrase "scripture is a conversation." So I prayed and played with it. I mused about how the books of Ezra and Jonah can be interpreted as a conversation, indeed a disagreement, and about how Paul dialogued with Peter on a two-week fact-finding trip to Jerusalem (Galatians 1:18), and then some fifteen years later had an embarrassing public quarrel with him in Antioch (Galatians 2:11-14). Bingo! Before I knew it, I had a verse:

> Scripture is a conversation,
> Ezra, Jonah, Peter, Paul;
> hidden is God's revelation,
> told to some, but meant for all.

1. George Caird, *New Testament Theology* (Oxford: Clarendon Press, 1994), p. 18: "The presupposition of our study is simply stated: to write a New Testament theology is to preside at a conference of faith and order. Around the table sit the authors of the New Testament, and it is the presider's task to engage them in a colloquium about theological matters which they themselves have placed on the agenda."

And then another verse, and another . . . —and then a hymn! Well, almost. Musically creative I am not, but I can follow a tune, so I found what seemed to me to be a suitable one, and then—yes—a hymn. Not exactly Brian Wren, but it would do, I thought, so I printed some copies, and "Scripture is a conversation" became our final hymn that Sunday evening.

After the service, one person said to me that she really liked the hymn. Hmm. When I got home I showed it to my wife, my most loyal supporter and my fiercest critic. "Not bad," she commented (high praise indeed!). "Show it to a colleague you respect." So I did. "I like it too," he said. "Show it to David Fox." David and I had been at Mansfield College, Oxford together. He had become an accomplished, published hymn-writer. Well, nothing ventured, nothing gained, so I emailed the hymn to David. His prompt response was very kind and encouraging.

And so I began writing hymns, usually composing them with a hymn-tune already in mind. Then on a long overdue three-month sabbatical I went on a tear, beginning to work my way through the liturgical year, and also to explore theologically some hot-button social and political issues. I needed advice and support—and I got it.

I corresponded with Fred Kaan and John Bell, who were immensely helpful. I regularly inflicted my work on my congregation, Bethel United Reformed Church, Swansea, who were receptive and responsive. I sent my hymns to the liturgical journal *Worship Live*, whose editor Janet Wootton welcomed my contributions and helped to hone my skills with her firm but gentle constructive criticism. I could always count on my good friend Steff Thomas (and her clever daughter Beth) to save me from composing intelligible, even poetic, but unfortunately unsingable verse. My daughter Katie not only patiently played tunes on her piano for her musically challenged Dad, she also bought me an album for my hymns, and, sweetly, a pack of little colored notes to stick beside them. My son plays the drums in bands with unmentionable names, so no help there, but WWKT—What Would Karl Think?—was a question that sometimes occurred to me as I teetered on the edge of cant or bathos. And, supremely, Angie, who for thirty-two years has been my partner in another kind of music-making, intrinsically improvisational, occasionally discordant, but finally wondrous beyond words—yes, marriage. God is a marvelous maestro.

Finally, if "Christ plays in ten thousand places" (Gerard Manley Hopkins), for the preparation of *Paddling* they include Sydney, Australia, where the outrageously gifted Ben Myers wrote the Foreword; Shrewsbury,

England, where my good friend and colleague Richard Hall did all the formatting, work which would have left this digitard not paddling but floundering; and Eugene, Oregon, where the good people at Wipf and Stock thought my hymns were worth publishing—and here we are.

I grew up by the seashore—in Huntington, New York—and I've spent my entire ministerial life by the seashore—in Swansea, Wales—so the Isaac Newton epigraph to this collection resonates for me geographically as well as theologically. But my hope, fellow paddlers, is that perhaps these hymns may embolden you to "push out further" (Luke 5:4) where—who knows?—you may find yourself winsomely worshipping with whales. As Cotton Mather playfully commanded:

> Ye monsters of the bubbling deep,
> Your Maker's praises spout;
> Up from the sands ye coddlings peep,
> And wag your tails about.

Foreword

NOTHING IS MORE DISTINCTIVE of the Christian faith than the habit of responding to God in song. There are other gods who require submission, obedience, and sacrifice; the God of Israel requires psalms of praise. There are other gods who elicit silence and mystical reveries; the God of Israel provokes the blowing of trumpets and the clashing of symbols. A huge portion of our scriptures are written in the form of poetry and song. Nearly all the Hebrew prophets were poets just as much as they were preachers. The song of Miriam and the song of Deborah are two of the oldest Hebrew texts to have found their way into our Old Testament. If one goes right back to the foundations of Israelite faith, one finds women singing and dancing and beating their tambourines in time.

In St Luke's account, the arrival of the Savior is greeted with a whole album of songs. The pregnant Mary sings, "My soul magnifies the Lord!" Zechariah has been struck mute throughout Elizabeth's pregnancy. But when the child is born, Zechariah's tongue is loosed and he bursts out singing: "Blessed be the Lord, the God of Israel!" When the birth of Jesus is near, the shepherds hear a multitude of angels singing: "Glory to God in the highest!" And when the baby is brought to the temple, old righteous Simeon takes the child in his arms and sings over him: "For mine own eyes have seen your salvation!" In St Luke's account of the birth of Christ, one feels that God has drawn so near that the whole creation is erupting spontaneously into song.

Some years ago I knew a woman in a nursing home who was in the most advanced stages of dementia. Her condition had worsened dramatically with the passing years. First she had forgotten her children; then she forgot her husband; then she forgot her own identity; then she forgot how to speak; then finally she forgot even her body so that she could no longer walk or eat or drink or do anything for herself. But one afternoon each week, a Salvation Army band would come to the nursing home. And the woman who had not spoken a word in years would sit in her wheelchair with a blank expression on her face while her mouth sang along to the old hymns. She had forgotten every Bible verse and every sermon she ever heard. She had forgotten whether she was a Calvinist or an Arminian, a conservative or a progressive. Yet when the band began to play, there were strings somewhere in the depths of her spirit that began to reverberate.

It is sobering to reflect that we will forget our loved ones, our children, even our own names, before we forget the songs that we have sung. Singing touches the nerve center of our lives. Our response to God comes from a place deeper even than ritual or belief. Indeed, as children many of us learned to sing about God—and therefore to love God—long before we ever began to think about God.

During his long pastoral ministry in Swansea, Kim Fabricius adopted the habit of writing hymns and encouraging his congregation to "sing a new song to the Lord" (Psalm 96:1). The hymns collected in this volume range across the heights and depths of the Christian story and Christian experience. There are hymns about doctrine, hymns about justice, hymns of anger and grief, hymns of careful reflection and hymns of simple childlike trust.

But the most striking thing about this songbook are the surprising flashes of humor on virtually every page. Hymn-writing is not traditionally a funny business. Most Christian hymns convey (or seek to convey) a note of spiritual solemnity: and the singing of hymns is often pretty hard work too. But the hymns of Kim Fabricius are marked by a sanctified frivolity and by a colloquialism reminiscent of Martin Luther's shamelessly popular approach to hymnody. I know of no other modern hymnbook in which one will find songs of praise set to the tunes of "Old MacDonald Had a Farm" and "Yankee Doodle Went to Town."

If praise touches the depths of the human spirit, these hymns remind us that praise does not require a specialized religious idiom. The language of praise is the language of ordinary life, for God meets us not in a special religious compartment of our lives but in the midst of ordinary day-to-day living. Every human experience can become an opportunity to pay attention to God and so to give God glory. If you ask me, that's something worth singing about—and as Kim reminds us in one of these hymns, "God is in the singing."

BENJAMIN MYERS
Sydney

God the Trinity

Eternal Father, almighty Father

Tune: *You Are My Sunshine*

Eternal Father, almighty Father,
you made the heavens and formed the earth;
you shaped all creatures
with winsome features,
and in time brought Jesus to birth.

Eternal Jesus, incarnate Jesus,
the one who sits at the Father's knee,
through human mother
became our brother,
lived and died for me, even me.

Eternal Spirit, life-giving Spirit,
love of the Father, love of the Son,
you live inside us
and safely guide us
through the Church to worlds yet to come.

O Liberator, Son, and Creator,
your very being in which we share
is bright and spacious,
and always gracious,
fill our hearts, Lord, with praises and prayer.

God is one, God is three

Tune: *Theodoric* – 666 66 with refrain

God is one, God is three,
not an "it", "he", or "she",
but a song, doh, ray, mi:
    God is in the singing,
    to the rhythm swinging:

      Take a chance, chance, chance,
      join the dance, dance, dance,
      sing the song,
      swing along,
      to the mystic music.

God is one, God is three,
the divine symphony,
love's the main melody:
    maestro of creation,
    orchestrates salvation:

God is one, God is three,
playing in harmony
music that sets us free:
    God is so surprising
    when he's improvising!

God is one, God is three,
infinite mystery,
touring in history:
    What a revelation!
    Give God an ovation!

For the love of God the Father

Tune: *Ar Hyd y Nos*

For the love of God the Father,
    we lift our hearts;
birthing children whom he mothers,
    we lift our hearts;
for his bold imagination
in the act of our creation,
and our wondrous variation,
    we lift our hearts.

For the grace of Christ eternal,
    we praise his name;
coming from his throne supernal,
    we praise his name;
for the challenge of his teaching,
for his hand to rebels reaching,
and the gates of hell all-breaching,
    we praise his name.

For the friendship of the Spirit,
    we sing our song;
irrespective of our merit,
    we sing our song;
for the living water gushing,
and the cooling breezes rushing,
full of force but never crushing,
    we sing our song.

God as Mystery

God is the deepest and blackest of holes

Tune: *Slane* – 10 10 10 11

God is the deepest and blackest of holes,
God is the eye-tooth that nibbles the soul,*
God is the wound that no surgeon can heal,
and God is the hub at the heart of the wheel.

God is the squatter who makes us his home,
God is the pest who won't leave us alone,
God is the boulder that lies in the way,
and God is the needle concealed in the hay.

God is the tiger that stalks us as prey,
God is the rash that will not go away,
God is the player who breaks all the rules,
and God is the wise one who acts like a fool.

God is the wrestler with arm round our throat,
God is the poison with no antidote,
God is the joker at wild in the deck,
and God is the king that no bishop can check.

God, you elude all our thinking and words—
eyes have not seen you and ears have not heard—
God, you're the Poet, we'll follow your way
by painting new pictures your self to portray.

---

* "The Tooth / That nibbles at the soul—" is the concluding line of Emily Dickinson's
poem "This World is not Conclusion."

God whose presence is an absence

Tune: *Servant Song* – 87 87 (Trochaic)

God whose presence is an absence,
    never like an object "there,"
speak to me in sounds of silence,
    in the voiceless void of prayer.

God whose truth's beyond all showing,
    not like one and one are two,
teach us truth's not known by knowing,
    truth is something that we do.

God whose being is an ocean,
    sea of love yet unexplored,
keep my flailing faith in motion
    as I paddle by the shore.

God who keeps a proper distance,
    God who runs ahead at pace,
leave us signs of your existence,
    footprints we may track and trace.

When in heaven we behold you,
    with the angels, face to face,
we will see that all we've been through
    was the trailer of your grace.

God in Creation and Providence

Out of nothing God created

Tune: *Blaenwern* – 87 87 D

Out of nothing God created
　　all the somethings that exist;
from a Bang the world inflated,
　　light-years later earth he kissed.
Starting with the smallest microbe,
　　moving from the sea to land,
life evolved around the new globe,
　　gently pushed by God's good hand.

"Go!" said God, and animated,
　　species spread by law and chance;
Spirit fashioned and related
　　each to all in sacred dance.
All that breathes is love's location,
　　not just humans in their pride;
by selection and mutation,
　　ask the beasts* how God can guide.

Now creation groans and shudders,
　　plundered, poisoned, colonized
by a beastly little brother,
　　self-styled as the one who's wise.
Will the sparrows finally perish,
　　though God clothes them and protects?
Time is short, so let us cherish
　　all that God will resurrect.

---

* "Ask the animals and they will teach you," says Job to his ignorant friends (Job 12:7)—
　　that's the biblical citation, but my inspiration here is Elizabeth Johnson and her won-
　　derful *Ask the Beasts: Darwin and the God of Love* (2014).

God the Father has a world

Tune: Old MacDonald Had a Farm

God the father has a world, E-I-E-I-O,
and in his world he has some stars, E-I-E-I-O:
with a "Light! Light!" here, and "Light! Light!" there,
here a "Light!", there a "Light!", everywhere a "Light" Light!";
God the Father has a world, E-I-E-I-O!

God the Father has a world, E-I-E-I-O,
and in his world he has an Earth, E-I-E-I-O:
with a "Live! Live!" here, and a "Live! Live!" there,
here a "Live!", there a "Live!", everywhere a "Live! Live!";
God the Father has a world, E-I-E-I-O!

God the Father has a world, E-I-E-I-O,
and in his world he has some folk, E-I-E-I-O:
with a "Mazel tov!"* here, and a "Mazel tov!" there,
here a "Mazel!", there a "tov!", everywhere a "Mazel tov!";
God the Father has a world, E-I-E-I-O!

God the Father has a world, E-I-E-I-O,
and in his world he has some prophets, E-I-E-I-O:
with "The Lord says!" here, and "The Lord says!" there,
here "He says!", there "He says!", everywhere "The Lord says!";
God the Father has a world, E-I-E-I-O!

God the Father has a world, E-I-E-I-O,
and in his world he has a Son, E-I-E-I-O:
with a "Peace! Peace!" here, and a "Peace! Peace!" there,
here a "Peace!", there a "Peace!", everywhere a "Peace! Peace!";
God the Father has a world, E-I-E-I-O!

God the Father has a world, E-I-E-I-O,
and in his world he has a church, E-I-E-I-O:
with an "Eat! Drink!" here, and an "Eat! Drink!" there,
here an "Eat!", there a "Drink!", everywhere an "Eat! Drink!";
God the Father has a church, E-I-E-I-O!

God the Father has a world, E-I-E-I-O,
and for his world he has a dream, E-I-E-I-O:
with a "Come, Lord!" here, and a "Come, Lord!" there,
here a "Come!", there a "Lord!", everywhere a "Come, Lord!";
God the Father has a world, E-I-E-I-O!

* "Mazel tov" is Yiddish for "Good luck."

God who creates and then colors the earth

Tune: *Here's to the Maiden*

God who creates and then colors the earth,
paints it with beautiful features—
oceans and islands, and forests and beasts—
preparing for reasoning creatures.

> *Sinful or pure, doubtful or sure,*
> *God comes to those who are ready or not;*
> *woman or male, healthy or frail,*
> *God wants us all to be part of the plot.*

God who calls Adam and Noah and Abe,
Moses and monarchs and seers,
fashions a people he claims for his own—
how odd!—in the land of Judea.

God who sends angels to Mary and Joe,
earthing the dream of Isaiah,
guides surprised shepherds and wise men to go
and witness the birth of Messiah.

God who empowers the Christ in his work,
scribes and disciples amazing,
sends his own Son to his suffering and death,
but saves the whole world by his raising.

God who continues his mission through saints—
folk overwhelmed by his glory;
still he is here after zillions of years
and writing us into his story.

Artful is God, creation is his canvas

Tune: *Som Stranden* – 11 10 11 10

Artful is God, creation is his canvas
    on which he paints his cosmic masterpiece:
brushstrokes both broad and delicate in detail,
    colors and shapes composed in perfect peace.

Artful is God, creation is his canvas
on which he paints his cosmic masterpiece.

Zillions of stars, exploding out of nothing,
    dance for the Lord, delightful in his eye;
billions of years it takes for sketching planets,
    time to design an earth to occupy.

Dazzling the sun, and silver-soft the moonlight,
    fruitful the land, and fathomless the sea;
wondrous is life, from single cell to primate,
    awesome is death, the final mystery.

What then of man, the end of evolution,
    image divine defaced by sin and vice?
Artful is God, producing from his palette
    Adam restored: self-portrait Jesus Christ!

God, in many ways you meet us

Tune: *Servant Song* – 87 87 (Trochaic)

God, in many ways you meet us,
    speak to us in world and church,
in the quake and in the quiet,
    when we flee and as we search.

In the splendor of the sunlight,
    in the sparkle of a star,
we see something of your glory,
    catch a glimpse of who you are.

On the canvas of an artist,
    in composer's sacred song,
through the verse and voice of poet,
    we sense worlds for which we long.

In the otherness of stranger
    and familiar face of friend,
we are entertaining angels
    whom your holy love commends.

When our lives are running smoothly,
    when our hopes have turned to dust,
through our joys and through our sorrows,
    in your providence we trust.

God, in word and wine we meet you
    in this sacramental space;
from the pulpit, on the table,
    close encounters with your grace.

Precious five the senses are*

Tune: *Humility* – 77 without refrain

Precious five the senses are,
how we find our way around
God's creation, near and far,
lengthways, sideways, up and down.

And we, using hearts and minds,
sounding depths and scaling heights,
logic-bound or unconfined,
navigate our way through life.

Conscience too directs our ways,
outer law and inner voice,
through the endless moral maze
with its agony of choice.

Yet with all these human skills,
sense and sensibility,
still we can't do what we will—
impotent ability.

Is there no way to release
old creation from its vice?
Look at what the Lord, by grace,
now has done in Jesus Christ!

God in peace invades the earth—
free at last from Satan's grip!—
triggers new creation's birth:
cruciform apocalypse!

* "Precious Five" is the title of a poem by W.H. Auden.

We look for God in nature's world

Tune: *Abingdon* – 88 88 88

We look for God in nature's world,
    for nature's world is from God's hand;
on earth expecting heaven unfurled,
    we scan the sky, the sea, the land:
but though we search with eye and mind,
the God we seek we cannot find.

We look for God in works of art,
    for works of art the Lord inspires;
speaking to human soul and heart,
    sparking a deep divine desire:
but though we search with eye and mind,
the God we seek we cannot find.

We look for God in moral sense,
    for moral sense the Lord instills;
in right and wrong the evidence
    for the Lawgiver's sovereign will:
but though we search with eye and mind,
the God we seek we cannot find.

God looks for us in God's own Son,
    in Jesus Christ, and Christ alone;
and at the cross the search is done,
    the lost are found and carried home:
our search for God?—we're blind as bats!—
like mice gone looking for a cat.*

So look for God in God's own Son,
    in Jesus Christ, and Christ alone;
no enterprise beneath the sun,
    nor any human knowledge known,
can ever show what God, by grace,
reveals to us in Jesus' face.

---

* In *Surprised by Joy*, C.S. Lewis wrote: "Amiable agnostics will talk cheerfully about 'man's search for God.' To me, as I then was, they might as well have talked about the mouse's search for the cat."

Christ's Advent and Birth

Are you the one who is to come?

Tune: *Dominus Regit Me* – 87 87 (Iambic)

Are you the one who is to come,
    or look we for another?
Will you arrive with doomsday drum,
    or peaceful like a brother?

Are you the Son who pardons sin,
    or look we for another?
Will you free us to breathe again,
    or with your judgment smother?

Are you the Christ to heal and bless,
    or look we for another?
Will you bring discord and distress,
    or comfort like a mother?

Are you the Lord whose love's free-range,
    or look we for another?
Will you embrace the odd and strange
    and altogether other?

You are the one, and now you're here,
    we look not for another;
Immanuel! With birthday cheer
we greet you like a brother.

It's Advent-time, our theme is hope

Tune: *Tallis's Canon* – LM

It's Advent-time, our theme is hope
    in Christ who comes to liberate;
don't scan the sky with telescopes,
    but watch the here and now—and wait.

The prophets listen for the word,
    and boldly speak the truth to power;
while people think it's quite absurd,
    the wealthy quake and tyrants cower.

The Baptist in the desert cries,
    "Repent, return, for heaven's sake!"
But to the rulers, with their lies,
    he says, "You vicious brood of snakes!"

An angel goes to Galilee,
    and tells a girl she's richly blessed:
"A virgin birth—how can this be?"
    the girl exclaims, but answers, "Yes!"

An angel visits Mary's man,
    and calms his fears about the birth:
Immanuel—God's cunning plan—
    to bring *shalom* to all the earth.

And so in time it comes to be:
    a baby's born who lives and dies,
he lives again for you and me,
    he comes again to dry all eyes.

In Mary's song of praise and peace

Tune: *University* – CM

In Mary's song of praise and peace
    we call "Magnificat,"
a peasant maiden mocked the claims
    of earth's proud plutocrats.

An angel whispered, "You're the one
    who'll carry heaven's child."
The girl, in fearful faith, said, "Yes!"
    but barely forced a smile.

She went to see a kindred soul,
    who praised what God would do;
yet Mary felt a deep unease
    about the coming coup.

But then she paused and prayed and thought,
    "Why am I full of doubt?
The Lord is good, I'll trust his ways,
    though they seem roundabout."

Her heart welled up, it overflowed
    with firm, determined joy,
because the Lord would save the world
    through such a subtle ploy.

"The poor will eat, parade the streets,"
    she sang, "and bands will play;
the pity is, with empty hands,
    the rich will rue the day."

Merry Christmas! Happy New Year!

Tune: *Sussex | Laus Deo* – 87 87 (Trochaic)

Merry Christmas! Happy New Year!
God's in heaven, all is well!
No, he's not, and all's not well here:
"God's on earth, but earth is hell."

Jolly families in December,
round the telly, watching *Morse*—
that's the image, but remember:
child abuse and bleak divorce.

Roof extension, central heating,
double glazing, sofa bed;
while the homeless, in the sleeting,
search for doorway, box, or shed.

British blood and UK passport,
porridge, Guinness, cawl, and tea—
this is our land, for our own sort:
no room for the refugee.

Bonus for the city slicker,
cuts in care for sick and old,
politicians strut and snicker:
same old story, newly told.

Tyrants—they will not enslave us;
terror—we will not condone;
but our formless fears deprave us:
now we hunt and kill with drones.

Jesus, we have come to greet you,
star-crossed child of midnight birth;
now we go to tell or tweet you:
"Earth is hell, but God's on earth!"

Happy birthday, baby Jesus

Tune: *Hyfrydol* – 87 87 D

Happy birthday, baby Jesus,
    born in awkward circumstance,
named in heaven "God is with us"
    while the world looked on askance.
You were praised by simple peasants,
    not by princes nor by priests.
Who should bring you priceless presents?
    Unbelievers from the East!

Son of Mary, girl unmarried,
    maid with soul who sang of peace,
with your father she was harried
    by Judea's thought police.
Boy delivered in a stable,
    tucked away behind an inn,
people libeled you with labels
    fixed by prejudice and sin.

Word of God for human reading,
    Holy Lord in fallen flesh,
one day you'll lie bruised and bleeding,
    cross stands waiting after crèche.
You confound all expectations,
    testing what we thought we knew;
deep Desire of all the Nations,
    exiles find their home in you.

Christmas and New Year

Tune: *Bunessan* – 54 54 D

Christmas and New Year,
    now they are over;
but all the good cheer—
    is it now past?
Yes, the big question—
    facing the future:
was it suggestion,
    or will it last?

Babies grow bigger,
    they become children;
boys in their vigor
    turn into men.
Will our love likewise
    grow to adulthood?
Can we the baptized
    answer "Amen"?

Child in the manger,
    safe and protected,
soon there'll be danger,
    conflict and loss.
We will go with you,
    Advent to Easter,
and we will stay true,
    cradle to cross.

Christ's Life and Ministry

A Jewish boy named Jesus

Tune: *The Incy Wincy Spider*

A Jewish boy named Jesus was born in Palestine,
    goys* came with gifts and shepherds saw a sign;
    soldiers were sent to disappear the child,
but an angel warned his father to flee into the wild.

The refugees returned, and the boy grew strong and wise,
    gathered disciples, preached and exorcized;
    sided with sinners, sought and found the lost,
so the great and good colluded to make him pay the cost.

Betrayed and handed over, the Judge was sent to trial,
    down in the courtyard, Peter in denial;
    up at the palace, Truth confronted Lie:
"What's the truth?" the Lie inquired, but the Truth did not reply.

They took the silent Word and they nailed him to a tree,
    dying, he spoke, "God, why abandon me?"
    Friends took the body, laid it in a cave,
while some guards were armed and posted to watch beside the grave.

The sleepy sentries dozed as the day began to dawn,
    women with spices came to weep and mourn;
    grief turned to fear, then joy, as angels said
that the Jesus they were seeking is risen from the dead.

The risen Christ continues to call us to proclaim:
    "Good News to all—salvation in my name!"
    Lord, off we go for all that we are worth,
as we join you in your project, renewing all the earth!

* "Goys" is a Jewish name for Gentiles.

There is a young rabbi

Tune: *Sweet Baby James*

There is a young rabbi, who preaches and heals,
    announcing the kingdom with gladness and glory,
    astonishing folk with his knack for a story,
told at a table while sharing a meal.
The rich ones don't like him—he curses their money;
    the poor ones adore him—he blesses their state;
the two-faced denounce him—he tells them they're phoney;
    the sinners revere him—he throws them a fête;
        he makes the afflicted feel great:

Praise God, you send us Jesus,
kindling the world with his flame;
he is the one who's uniquely your Son,
the one whom all Christians proclaim.
Praise God for his wonderful name!

Now the first Maundy Thursday, he washes our feet;
    he feeds us, then leaves us for cruel condemnation;
    he wrestles the devil and offers oblation,
when on the cross he goes down to defeat.
The soldiers, they sleep, as they guard the dead body;
    the women, they weep, as they go to the tomb;
the angels, they laugh, "Are you seeking somebody?
    He's not here, he's risen and scattered the gloom;
        salvation now blossoms and blooms!"

Praise God, you send us Jesus,
kindling the world with his flame;
he is the one who's uniquely your Son,
the one whom all Christians proclaim.
Praise God for his wonderful name!

Baptized and Spirit-driven

Tune: *Aurelia* – 76 76 D

Baptized and Spirit-driven,
    our Lord went forth inspired,
for all the unforgiven
    to face the Satan's fire;
he wrestled the temptation
    for agonizing hours,
of gaining our salvation
    through soul-corrupting power.

He tested his vocation
    with ruthless honesty,
without equivocation
    he probed his inner "me";
he fought his desert demons,
    he battled with his beasts,
they left him for a season,
    but did not leave in peace.

The devil bashed the Bible,
    appealed to common sense;
but Jesus saw the libel:
    "Go, Satan, get thee hence!"
No, Lord, you weren't exempted
    from Adam's awful plight;
be there when we are tempted,
    our forty days and nights.

Jesus talked with Gentiles

Tune: *North Coates* – 65 65

Jesus talked with Gentiles,
    shook the status quo;
praised a Roman captain
    though he was a foe.

Jesus played with children,
    shook the status quo;
criticized disciples
    when they cried out, "No!"

Jesus touched the scabby,
    shook the status quo;
and he healed a blind man
    down in Jericho.

Jesus honored women,
    shook the status quo;
took them from the kitchen,
    put them in the know.

Jesus ate with outcasts,
    shook the status quo;
told the sinners, "Welcome!",
    told the righteous, "Woe!"

Jesus mixed with all sorts,
    shook the status quo:
All our cruel exclusions
    finally have to go!

Christ's Passion and Death

Jesus goes from Jericho

Tune: *Yankee Doodle Went to Town*

Jesus goes from Jericho,
    behind him Bartimaeus;
next stop town of Bethany,
    the last will be Emmaus.

    Praise to Jesus—wave your palms!—
    masterful in meekness,
    Prince of Peace who comes unarmed
    and wins the world through weakness!

Jesus nears Jerusalem
    and looks upon the city,
sees it won't give peace a chance
    and weeps a tear of pity.

Jesus sends two friends ahead
    to get a donkey ready;
at the city gates the mood
    is cheerful, charged, and heady.

Jesus enters on the colt,
    the crowd goes wild with cheering,
waving branches, spreading cloaks,
    no hint of mutineering.

Jesus sees some Pharisees,
    their faces pursed and pouting;
"Were the people dumb," he says,
    "the pavement would be shouting!"

So begins the Holy Week,
    a day of benediction;
who would ever have believed
    by Friday—crucifixion.

Jesus entering the city

Tune: *Quem Pastores Laudavere* – 888 7

Jesus entering the city
on a donkey, grand but gritty,
weeping tears of peace and pity—
    rocks and stones cannot be dumb.

Jesus at the place of praying,
overturning tables, saying,
"In my Father's house no paying!"—
    now the Temple's Judge has come.

Jesus in the Temple preaching,
using stories for his teaching,
Pharisees and scribes are screeching,
    while the traitor does his sums.

Jesus breaking bread at table
with the friends that he's enabled—
"Who's the greatest?"—speech of Babel—
    fit not even for the crumbs.

Jesus in the garden crying,
"Spare me from this dreadful dying!"
God is silent—terrifying!—
    but the Savior won't succumb.

Jesus at his execution
starts religion's revolution,
end of violent retribution—
    victim victor now becomes.

Jesus kneels down, Peter reels round

Tune: *Infant Holy* – 447D 4444 77

Jesus kneels down,
Peter reels round
as he's told to take a seat.
Jesus hushes,
Peter blushes
at the Lord who washes feet.
Role reversal,
a unique play,
dress rehearsal
for the Friday:
Praise the God of bowl and cross!
Praise the God of bowl and cross!

Back at table,
still unstable,
friends of Jesus reconstrue.
Reprimanded,
now commanded,
"Do what I have done for you!"
Love's portrayal
while they're eating;
Christ's betrayal—
self-defeating:
Reigns the God of bowl and cross!
Reigns the God of bowl and cross!

Pilate poses, Christ exposes

Tune: *Infant Holy* – 447D 4444 77

Pilate poses,
Christ exposes—
power challenged and defied;
Christ appearing,
people jeering—
sin and righteousness collide.
Life the winner,
new creation;
for the sinner
full salvation:
Christ the Lord is crucified!
Christ the Lord is crucified!

'Midst the shambles
soldiers gamble,
bandits braying at his side;
earth is shaken,
dead awaken
at the dreadful deicide.
An absurd day—
wait!—surprises!—
on the third day
Jesus rises:
Christ the Lord is glorified!
Christ the Lord is glorified!

Beneath an unforgiving sky

Tune: *The House of the Rising Sun / Amazing Grace* – CM

Beneath an unforgiving sky
    hangs Christ, the Father's Son;
"Forgive them, Father," hear him cry,
    "they don't know what they've done."

Two hang with Christ upon the tree
    (while soldiers play at dice);
"Today"—his promise—"you will be
    with me in paradise."

A friend stands, dumb with disbelief,
    the one who did not run;
his mother too stands numb with grief—
    he says, "Behold, your son."

In agony and deep distress,
    adrift on howling seas,
he hurls a frantic SOS,
    "God, why abandon me?"

The fount of healing streams who said,
    though men might do their worst,
he'd feed us with the living bread,
    now simply says, "I thirst."

The day grows dark, the end draws near,
    nails tearing hands and feet,
he shouts in triumph, loud and clear,
    "Now everything's complete!"

He bows his head, "My God, I give
    my soul into your hands."
The seed is sown—to die, to live—
    O who can understand?

Christ's Resurrection, Reign, and Saving Work

In the graveyard Christ appeared

Tune: *Puer Nobis* – 76 77 Irregular

In the graveyard Christ appeared,
    reaching out to Mary,
wiped her tears and calmed her fears—
    disciples, they were wary. *[Repeat.]*

Christ on the Emmaus Road
    gave two his attention,
yet another episode
    of blind incomprehension.

Jesus in the upper room
    late that Sunday evening,
friends still filled with doom and gloom—
    they hadn't got the meaning.

Seven days, and Thomas too,
    in doubt and deep dejection,
showed he didn't have a clue
    about the resurrection.

By the lakeside—Christ again!—
    after celebration,
questioned Peter there and then
    about his dedication.

Still disciples ask today,
    "Was it an illusion?"
Holy Spirit, chase away
    our muddle and confusion.

Jesus is risen

Tune: *Addington* – 54 54 D

Jesus is risen,
    raised by the Father,
and the imprisoned
    rise in his train;
hell has been harrowed,
    evil defeated;
humankind hallowed,
    shares in his reign.

Jesus is living,
    ruling in heaven
through his forgiving
    people on earth;
churches in mission
    groan with creation,
hastening fruition,
    cosmic rebirth.

Jesus is coming,
    time for rejoicing,
heavens are humming,
    planets and stars;
foes are befriended,
    friends are astonished,
hands are extended,
    bearing the scars.

Then Jesus, handing
    over the kingdom—
everyone standing,
    cheering the Lord—
gives all his glory
    back to the Father,
ending the story
    scripture records.

Lord Jesus Christ, your mighty resurrection

Tune: *Charterhouse* – 11 10 11 10

Lord Jesus Christ, your mighty resurrection
    fills us with overwhelming joy and fear,
as you begin your world-wide insurrection,
    and lead the way as faith's great pioneer.

Your cross proclaims the depths of our corruption,
    your empty tomb the heights of grace sublime,
your risen power causes an eruption
    of love exploding out through space and time.

You lived a life of challenge, trust, and service,
    you suffered death in doubt and agony,
you live again and stride ahead with purpose,
    and bring your friends along for company.

As risen Lord, you call us all to mission,
    embracing people, creatures, earth, and stars,
you give to each a personal commission
    to share your healing as we bear your scars.

Exalted Christ, the victim's vindication,
    we follow in the slipstream you release,
propelled by promise of the new creation
    when the whole universe will be at peace.

Imagine all the countless ways

Tune: *Gonfalon Royal* – LM

Imagine all the countless ways
    that picture how the Savior saves.
We lift our hearts in thanks and praise
    for cruel cross and empty grave.

He draws together Greek and Jew,
    he razes walls and ends all strife;
not for a pre-selected few,
    but for the world he gives his life.

He pays the ransom, setting free
    the slaves of sin and selfishness;
he liberates us all to be
    the slaves of grace and righteousness.

He gives himself in sacrifice,
    unblemished lamb for sinners slain;
he gives himself, while men play dice,
    to expiate the crime of Cain.

He puts us right when we are wrong,
    as judge he takes the felon's place;
released disciples sing a song—
    the prosecution has no case.

Lord, finish now the world you planned—
    perfecting is the Spirit's art—
the world in Christ that you began,
    the world you love with all your heart.
        (Amen.)

The Holy Spirit

Holy Spirit, breath of life

Tune: *Gwalchmai* – 74 74 D

Holy Spirit, breath of life,
    breathe upon me;
comforter in times of strife,
    make my fears flee.
You alone can save my soul
    from life's wild sea;
you alone can fill the hole
    deep within me.

Come, then, Spirit from above,
    fall upon me;
bond of Son and Father's love,
    set my soul free.
To the cell in which I'm bound
    you're the sole key;
through the years you've sought and found
    self-enclosed me.

God of warmth who goes between
    others and me;
God of light who can't be seen,
    help us to see:
only as we live in you
    can we then be;
living then for others too,
    I become me.

Holy Spirit, sudden gust

Tune: *Kelvingrove* – 76 76 7776

Holy Spirit, sudden gust
  and darting tongue of flame,
one whose presence is a must
  or worship's limp and lame,
as we gather here to meet,
come and sweep us off our feet,
where we're cold, turn up the heat—
  it's new creation time!

Holy Spirit, gentle dove,
  all-animating breath,
you bear fruit in peace and love,
  you bring life out of death,
draw together those apart
with your reconciling art,
stimulate the stony heart—
  it's new creation time!

Holy Spirit, one of three,
  the God who goes between,
you declared the Jubilee
  through God the Nazarene,
through the church communicate
words and deeds that liberate,
and the world will be a fête—
  it's new creation time!

The Holy Scriptures

Scripture is a conversation

Tune: *Servant Song* – 87 87 (Trochaic)

Scripture is a conversation,
Ezra, Jonah, Peter, Paul;
hidden is God's revelation,
told to some but meant for all.

Like a conference, many speakers
vie to make their voices heard;
only to the eyes of seekers
is disclosed the living Word.

We are called to be discerning
as we eavesdrop on the text;
not for answers but for learning
may the Spirit richly vex.

Move me from my fixed opinions,
axe laid to the frozen sea*;
Lord, I long for your dominion,
liberated from my "me."

Thus unthreatened by the other,
unconcerned with being wrong,
may we add with sister, brother,
to your all-inclusive song.

* In a letter to Oskar Pollak, Franz Kafka wrote: "A book must be the *axe* for the *frozen sea* inside us."

Let us listen for the Word

Tune: *Buckland / Vienna* – 77 77

Let us listen for the Word,
as we hear it read and preached,
sharper than the sharpest sword,
sweeter than the sweetest peach.

Scripture sings in different keys—
hymns of praise and mournful cries,
letters, legends, histories,
guidance from the worldly-wise.

Written with imperfect scores,
pitched for people culture-bound,
scarred by old barbaric laws—
scripture makes discordant sounds.

Yet a love-song, with refrain,
resonates from all around;
sunshine breaks through cloud and rain,
flowers bloom from barren ground.

God, whose Word is cruciform,
as we hear it preached and read,
may our hearts be strangely warmed,*
and our souls raised from the dead.

---

* The reference, of course, is to John Wesley reflecting on his Aldersgate Street experience: "I felt my heart strangely warmed."

Praise and Prayer

Make haste, God's grace

Make haste, God's grace
is now in this place:

> *Jesus shared with his,*
> *Jesus cared with his,*
> *Jesus dared with his friends!*

Come in, begin—
forgiven is sin:

Relent, repent—
the Spirit is sent:

Be stirred—the Word
is spoken and heard:

This way to pray:
"Tomorrow today!":

In line to dine—
true bread and new wine:

Go out, and shout
what God is about:

Why do people go to church?

Tune: Kelvingrove – 76 76 7776

Why do people go to church?
    Why do we worship God?
While our neighbors lie in bed,
    why do we act so odd?
As we fold our hands and pray,
as we hear what preachers say,
as we pass around the tray,
    we would *become* the church.

Why do people go to church?
    Why do we get enthused?
While our neighbors work or play,
    why do we pack the pews?
As we sing our psalms and songs,
as we learn what's right and wrong,
as we try to get along,
    we would *become* the church.

Why do people go to church?
    Why do we offer praise?
While our neighbors sit in pubs,
    why do we stand amazed?
As forgiven we forgive,
as in gratitude we give,
as we practise how to live,
    we would *become* the church.

Here's why Christians come to church:
    because we've heard the call,
we're responding to the grace
    of God, the Lord of all.
We're not here because we choose,
we're not here to be amused,
we are here to hear Good News
    and so to *be* the church.

Prayer the church's fast and feast

Tune: *England's Lane / Heathlands* – 77 77 77

[in homage to the poem "Prayer" by George Herbert]

Prayer the church's fast and feast,
    recipes for grief and praise;
prayer the creature's common speech,
    mind and soul in paraphrase:

> *Father God, how good to share*
> *all our love and pain and care.*

Prayer the land of sun and spice,
    hearts on holiday abroad;
prayer the blood of sacrifice,
    blessed spear that pierced our Lord:

Prayer the compass of desire,
    pointing to the promised rest;
prayer the truth against the liar,
    passing all the devil's tests:

Prayer the token of the best,
    poetry of cheerful rhymes;
prayer the sound of deep unrest,
    thunderclaps for tempest-times:

Prayer the ear that hears the tones,
    sounding from angelic spheres;
prayer the voice that moves the stone,
    pressing on the tomb of years:

Prayer the raising of the dead,
    turning evil into good;
prayer the way the world is read,
    sense of something understood:

Lord, behold a wretched sinner

Tune: *Quem Pastores Laudavere* – 888 7

Lord, behold a wretched sinner,
from the outer to the inner;
at repentance, rank beginner:
    day and night my conscience cries.

Where begin? My faults keep mounting;
when I start I can't stop counting;
huge the sum, but Christ's accounting
    crosses out and nullifies.

Good I would but can't achieve it,
bad I hate but can't relieve it.
God for us? I can't believe it:
    me, the apple of his eye!

God forgives before petition;
grace alone shows our condition;
truth demands our self-suspicion:
    like a snake the heart is sly.

While accusing scribes are hissing,
Christ portrays the Father kissing
cheek of child that he's been missing:
    Love forgives and sanctifies!

The Sacraments

O what a happy day!

Tune: *Franconia / Carlisle* – SM

O what a happy day!
We celebrate a death—
a dying into Jesus Christ—
a girl's/boy's re-birth by Breath!

All sin is washed away,
now all is undefiled.
The Lord says, "I will be your God,
and you will be my child."

Incorporate in Christ,
and by the Spirit sealed,
this girl/boy will have a special place
reserved for holy meals.

Her/His bondage now is past,
an exodus begins,
a pilgrimage in company
of Christian kith and kin.

This family of God,
by water and the Word,
may all be found at journey's end
as faithful as our Lord.

Let's have a meal, let's have a feast!

Tune: *Truro* – LM

Let's have a meal, let's have a feast!
    Come one and all, from great to least:
the food and drink have been prepared,
    the Lord provides and all is shared.

Let's have a meal, let's have a feast!
    This table cannot be policed:
it's not the church's, it's the Lord's,
    it's spread for free, not for reward.

Let's have a meal, let's have a feast!
    From "us" and "them" we've been released:
no strangers here, for all are friends,
    no need to hide, deride, defend.

Let's have a meal, let's have a feast!
    Join hearts and hands, and pass the peace:
Christ turned the cheek and walked the mile,
    now all to each are reconciled.

Let's have a meal, let's have a feast!
    Let grace abound, let joy increase!
And as we take the bread and wine,
    let who we are be re-defined.

Discipleship and Pilgrimage

God of all ages, ageless Lord

Tune: *Ombersley* – LM

God of all ages, ageless Lord,
whose thoughts are deep, whose love is broad,
we of all ages offer praise
throughout the length of all our days.

We praise you for our wondrous birth,
formed from your breath and blessed earth,
shaped in the womb by your own hand—
miracle!—who can understand?

We praise you for the years of youth,
time to explore the realms of truth,
stretching our muscles and our minds,
testing new models of mankind.

We praise you for our grown-up years,
with their demands, their joys and fears;
taking the world you give in trust,
working to make it fair and just.

We praise you for retiring age,
as we approach life's final page;
still things to do, still sights to see,
but, most of all, we learn to be.

This is our life, from birth to death,
from infant's cry to final breath;
this is our life, our gift to you,
who gave it first, who'll make it new.

Lord, we thank you for tradition

Tune: *Drakes Broughton* – 87 87 (Trochaic)

Lord, we thank you for tradition,
    for the Fathers and the Creeds,
for Reformers' erudition,
    speaking to the church's needs.

And we thank you for their power
    to transcend a single time,
pressing on the present hour
    with still fruitful paradigms.

But, Lord, save us from supposing
    that our calling's to repeat
what the church once said, so closing
    minds to truths yet incomplete.

Teach us, Lord, the past's potential
    for creation, not control,
lest we, seeking what's essential,
    take the partial for the whole.

When we see your glory blazing,
    our best thoughts will seem like straw*;
how can human words and phrasing
    capture God who's always more?

---

* Three month before he died, Thomas Aquinas had a revelatory experience. Afterwards he said, "I can write no more. All that I have written seems like straw to me."

God's church is a school for learning

Tune: *Bethany* – 87 87 D

God's church is a school for learning,
    life-long learning in the Lord;
here we're taught to be discerning
    as we read and hear his Word.
Taught to dramatize the Story,
    Christians all have parts to play
in the theater of his glory,
    improvising on the way.

In the church of God are courses
    in the arts of peace and prayer,
and in using the resources
    from the files of love and care;
classes in the craft of living,
    seminars on grace and sin,
Sunday workshops in forgiving,
    coaching by the Christ within.

Thinking thoughts of God—what wonder!—
    trained in virtue, given space,
we will make mistakes and blunder,
    still in church there's always place:
place for all—here no exclusions—
    place for each—the fast and slow;
here we see through sight's illusions,
    here by faith alone we know.

We're the family of God

Tune: *Kelvingrove* – 76 76 7776

We're the family of God,
    and we are richly blessed
with traditions that are odd—
    including fancy dress!
But in Jesus we are one—
deacon, steward, priest, or nun—
though our journey's just begun
    to be the coming Church.

We are Baptist and Reformed,
    we're Catholic and Friend,
for there is no single norm,
    we need a special blend
to exalt and praise the Lord
in the silence, wine, and word—
but we sound a common chord
    to sing the coming Church.

As we gather here today
    to mark the Week of Prayer,
in commitment to the Way
    that leads from here to there,
may our worship well express
that the Christ whom we confess
is the goal to which we press
    to be the coming Church.

When our time together ends,
    it's then the service starts,
as the Holy Spirit sends
    us out to play our part:
may we hasten from this place
to the waiting human race
with the joyful news of grace,
    and be the coming Church.

The church of God is always slow

Tune: *Melcombe* – LM

The church of God is always slow
    to follow where the Spirit leads;
a pilgrim people on the go,
    yet hesitant to move at speed.

We meet in councils and debate,
    we keep the church in good repair,
we manage and administrate,
    but have no time to dream and dare.

We sit in buildings all aloof,
    remembering the days of yore;
we're more concerned about the roof
    than hunger, justice, peace, and war.

And why begrudge the Spirit's work
    outside the church, among the throng?
Or is it only Christian folk
    who speak the truth and right the wrong?

Confess, the church is out of touch,
    we're all at sea, becalmed, marooned.
Repent, for God is not a crutch,
    and not a bandage but the wound.*

O Holy Spirit, burn and blow,
    and drive us on, full steam ahead;
no turning back, no contraflow,
    but constant rising from the dead.

---

* In March 1994, three months before his death from cancer, the British playwright Dennis Potter gave a television interview in which he said, "For me, religion is the wound, not the bandage."

Do I love God? How can I know?

Tune: *St. Fulbert* – CM

Do I love God? How can I know?
    By following the rules?
No, rules are guides that can't divide
    the faithful from the fool.

Do I love God? How can I know?
    By keeping to the creeds?
No, right belief brings no relief
    from doubts that grow like weeds.

Do I love God? How can I know?
    By looking deep within?
No, introspection's always marred
    by self-deceit and sin.

Do I love God? How can I know?
    I can't, but I can trust
the God whose grace I can't escape,
    whose judgment's more than just.

Do I love God? How can I know?
    I can't—but here's the key:
I love God only as I love
    the ones who don't love me.

Where, we ask, is God today?

Tune: *Emma* – 77 77

Where, we ask, is God today—
    in the gaps that science leaves,
    gaps that close as knowledge grows?
Such a God is on reprieve.

Where, we ask, is God today—
    in the private place of prayer,
    where we find security?
Such a God's a teddy bear.

Where, we ask, is God today—
    in the church, behind its walls,
    for a cause in quarantine?
Such a God is far too small.

Where, we ask, is God today—
    in jihad or cruel crusade,
    in the council room of war?
Such a God's the devil's aide.

Where, we ask, is God today—
    in the questions that we ask,
    in the puzzles and the pain?
God is in the toils and tasks!

Where, we ask, is God today—
    are we where his Christ would be,
    with the outcast and ignored?
Such is God's humanity!

Who are we called to be?

Tune: *Moscow* – 664 6664

Who are we called to be?
The Father's family—
    greatest is least.
Sisters and brothers, pray
for bread and peace today,
and for the poor that they
    share in the feast.

Who are we called to be?
The Son's community—
    song, salt, and light.
Become what Christ became,
witness to Yahweh's reign,
go set the world aflame—
    God's dynamite!

Who are we called to be?
The Spirit's colony—
    exiles and clowns.
Live as the dispossessed,
free of the fear of death,
heal hate with tenderness—
    world upside-down!

Children die from drought and earthquake

Tune: *Scarlet Ribbons* – 87 87 D

Children die from drought and earthquake,
    children die by hand of man.
What on earth, and what for God's sake,
    can be made of such a plan?
Nothing—no such plan's been plotted;
    nothing—no such plan exists:
if such suffering were allotted,
    God would be an atheist.

Into ovens men drive "others,"
    into buildings men fly planes;
history's losers are the mothers,
    history's winners are the Cains.
Asking where was God in Auschwitz,
    or among the Taliban:
God himself was on the gibbets—
    thus the question: Where was man?

God of love and God of power—
    attributes in Christ are squared.
Faith can face the final hour,
    doubt and anger can be aired.
Answers aren't in explanation,
    answers come at quite a cost:
only wonder at creation,
    and the practise of the cross.

Justice and Shalom

Christ is Lord of all creation

Tune: *Rhuddlan* – 87 87 87

Christ is Lord of all creation,
    rules the universe in peace;
brings to judgment every nation
    which would be the world's police:
Lamb of God who lies with lions,
    slain, he conquers Babel's beast.

Weapons used for mass destruction,
    tools deployed in torture cell—
horror shows of sheer revulsion
    scripted, acted, shot in hell:
Where is God? Not hid in heaven,
    here, in blood—Immanuel!

In this world of fear and violence,
    in the teeth of hate and death;
courage, Christian, and defiance
    till your faithful final breath:
in our deeds and proclamation—
    "God is love!" our shibboleth.

Praise to Jesus in the kitchen

Tune: *Oh My Darling, Clementine*

Praise to Jesus in the kitchen,
in a mansion or a flat,
pitch or pub or children's playpen—
where we are is where he's at.

In the boardroom and the City,
on the dole and in the slums,
here in judgment, there in pity,
suddenly the Savior comes.

With the sick, and sad, and lonely,
in the hospice, on the street,
Servant Son, the one and only,
kneels and washes weary feet.

Concentration camps and prisons,
scenes of torture and despair,
sickening sights on television:
pick a place—the Lord is there!

Into death and hell descending,
Christ the fellow-sufferer goes,
purges pain that seems unending,
knots the fire and the rose.*

High in heaven, Christ ascended,
far beyond the farthest stars,
no one, nowhere, unbefriended—
where he's at is where we are!

*All manner of thing shall be well
 When the tongues of flame are in-folded
 Into the crowned knot of fire
 And the fire and the rose are one
 —T. S. Eliot, "Little Gidding"

Imagine a world

Tune: *Streets of Laredo*

Imagine a world where our leaders aren't liars,
    distorting reporting and spinning the news;
where all whistle-blowers and brave Jeremiahs
    are lauded, applauded, and never abused.

Imagine a world where believers aren't fighting
    and shedding our blood in the name of their gods;
where faith is delightful, enlightening, inviting,
    and never deployed for crusades or jihads.

Imagine a world where the markets aren't idols,
    bowed down to and worshipped in envy and greed;
where wealth is released and the bankers are bridled,
    the poor have a plot and the famished a feed.

Imagine a world where there is no pollution,
    the air is so clear and the oceans are clean;
where humans don't threaten the earth's evolution,
    the animals flourish and forests are green.

Imagine a world as the Lord has intended,
    where goodness and justice and beauty preside;
a world we have broken that might yet be mended:
    the future is now, it is ours to decide.

O God of peace

Tune: *Sine Nomine* – 10 10 10 with Alleluias

O God of peace, whose peace is Christ your Son,
put on your armor that the war be won,
the war on war, your Word against the gun:
    Allelulia! Allelulia!

O God of power, whose power appears so weak,
call up your soldiers from among the meek,
who won't turn tail, but turn the other cheek:
    Allelulia! Allelulia!

O God of love, whose love casts out all fear,
steady your people when the warlike jeer,
but rather insults than their blood and tears:
    Allelulia! Allelulia!

O God of hosts, whose host is bread for life,
feed us by faith for strength in times of strife,
and fill with hope the grieving child and wife:
    Allelulia! Allelulia!

O God of time, whose time is always nigh,
keep us alert to leaders' lethal lies,
come now your reign when truth will never die:
    Allelulia! Allelulia!

Peter was a hothead

Tune: *North Coates* – 65 65

Peter was a hothead,
    Jesus loved him still,
let him see his glory
    high upon a hill.

Matthew was a taxman,
    Jesus loved him still,
partied at his table,
    ate and drank his fill.

Simon was a rebel,
    Jesus loved him still,
and replaced his dagger
    with a daffodil,

Judas was a traitor,
    Jesus loved him still,
even when he kissed him
    in the midnight chill.

Thomas was a doubter,
    Jesus loved him still,
let him touch the nail holes
    when his faith was nil.

All of us are sinners,
    Jesus loves us still,
let us show we love him
    as we do his will.

In Christ we're neither nor

Tune: *Carlisle* – SM

In Christ we're neither nor,
    for all in Christ are one;
Christ is himself the open door
    through whom the nations come.

In Christ no Greek nor Jew,
    as oppositions fall
before the one who twins the two
    by breaking down the wall.

In Christ no slave nor free,
    now all are slaves to each,
and equal in his company
    the greatest and the least.

In Christ no he and she,
    so men may now be meek,
while women hold apostles' keys
    and bear the worn and weak.

In Christ no black nor white,
    for God is color-kind;
all human hues the Lord invites
    to feasts of bread and wine.

In Christ no straight nor gay,
    and we shall overcome
this final fear that blocks the day
    we dream of coming home.

In Christ we're neither nor,
    for all in Christ are one.
Sing praise to Christ the open door
    through whom all nations come!

How beautiful the human race

Tune: *University* – CM

How beautiful the human race
    in mind and soul and heart,
but also for the body's grace*
    we praise the Maker's art.

From head to toe God made us fair,
    a wonder to perceive,
as Adam saw when first he stared
    and fell in love with Eve.

The tender touch, the ardent kiss,
    the trembling deep within—
such passion is the body's bliss
    and not a shameful sin.

Repent, O Church, for all the dirt
    we've dumped on natural joys,
and for the burden and the hurt
    of guilt that we've deployed.

Let love be bold to speak its name,
    let flesh not fear the fire,
since flesh the Son of God became,
    we celebrate desire.

* "The Body's Grace" is the title of the 10th Michael Harding Memorial Address given by Rowan Williams in 1989.

We hang our heads in shame and guilt

Tune: *Mit Freuden Zart* – 87 87 887

We hang our heads in shame and guilt
　　for ruthless exploitation:
we heat the earth and watch it wilt
　　for capital and nation.
In pitiless pursuit of oil
we poison air and sea and soil—
　　the lords of de-creation.

"Have mercy on us, Lord!" we plead,
　　but is it false confession?
We mask misdeeds, we gild our greed,
　　as peace we spin aggression.
We're skillful at the apt excuse,
and the dark arts of word-abuse—
　　the truth is in recession.

O God, this is our world of vice,
　　come, judge us, test us, try us;
though we deny you, Jesus Christ,
　　Deliverer, don't deny us;
break down the selves in which we hide,
evict our vanity and pride—
　　O Spirit, occupy us!

Migrant Jesus, at the border

Tune: *Drakes Broughton*

Migrant Jesus, at the border,
refugee of fear and hate,
you're a threat to law and order,
nightmare of the nation-state.

Child of Israel, fleeing soldiers,
from the Jordan to the Nile,
were your parents passport-holders,
were you welcomed with a smile?

Home from Egypt, Spirit-breathing,
in the towns of Galilee,
how you had the people seething
when you preached the Jubilee.

At the margins, far from center,
where you met the ostracized,
even friends weren't keen to enter
conversations that you prized.

Ease our fears, forgive our hatred
of the other and the odd;
help us see the single-sacred:
face of stranger—face of God.

Migrant Jesus, at the border—
Dover Beach or Rio Grande—
Greetings, sister! Welcome, brother!
Make this place your promised land.

The Christian Hope

Death comes in many forms

Tune: *Franconia* – SM

Death comes in many forms,
  it comes to young and old,
it comes as friend and enemy—
  its ways are manifold.

It comes as sudden shock,
  it comes as soothing sleep,
it comes at dawn and noon and dusk
  its final tryst to keep.

It comes in quake and plague,
  it comes by knife and gun,
it creeps up when we least expect
  and switches off the sun.

It comes alone, aloof,
  it comes in suit and tie,
it comes as though it knows it all
  yet cannot tell us why.

Is death the mastermind?
  Is death the perfect thief?
Are shock and anger and despair
  his plunder from our grief?

A pyrrhic victory!
  "O death, where is your sting?"
Eternal life is ours in Christ,
  our risen, conquering King!

What happens after death?

Tune: *Gildas / St. Michael* – SM

What happens after death?
Will humans live again?
Is nothingness the destiny
that marks our final end?

Does heaven lie above?
Is hell a pit of fire?
Do all get just what they deserve
or what their hearts desire?

What happens after death?
Of course we live again!
From nothingness God spoke his word
of life—and life's our end.

Yes, heaven is a place,
but not a place above,
it's found in God's geography,
located in his love.

And, yes, there is a hell,
a state of black despair,
but Christ assumes what we deserve,
so not a soul is there.

Our hope is Christ alone,
divine humanity,
who lived and died and lives again
for all eternity.

www.ingramcontent.com/pod-product-compliance
Lightning Source LLC
Chambersburg PA
CBHW071102090426
42737CB00013B/2438